Mean

KEN BABSTOCK

Mean

Poems

Anansi

Published in 1999 by
House of Anansi Press Limited
34 Lesmill Road, Toronto, ON
Canada M3B 2T6
Tel. (416) 445-3333
Fax (416) 445-5967
www.anansi.ca

Distributed in Canada by
General Distribution Services Inc.
325 Humber College Blvd., Etobicoke, ON
Canada M9W 7C3
Tel. (416) 213-1919
Fax (416) 213-1917
E-mail Customer.Service@ccmailgw.genpub.com

03 02 01 00 99   1 2 3 4 5

CANADIAN CATALOGUING IN PUBLICATION DATA
Babstock, Ken, 1970–
Mean

Poems.
ISBN 0-88784-634-3

PS8553.A245M42 1999   C811'.54   C98-933054–0
PR9199.3B285M42 1999

Cover design: Angel Guerra
Printed and bound in Canada
Typesetting: ECW Type & Art, Oakville

*House of Anansi Press gratefully acknowledges the Canada Council
for the Arts, the Government of Canada through the Book
Publishing Industry Development Program (BPIDP), and the
Ontario Arts Council for their support of our publishing program.*

*This first one is for David O'Meara,
another pussycat from that bad town,
whose hand I felt upon my hand at
every word.*

CONTENTS

Means

Head Injury Card

Measures

MEANS

You cannot count on his face enduring.

He has retreated into savagery.

It is not easy to report this.
— Don Coles

Don't say you don't know what I mean. You've seen me there.
— Andrew Motion

Camping at Glendalough

A goat-track, for hours, a gorse-edged trough
that fanned to a dusted bristle of heather.
We pitched our pegless tent on the crest
where it lifted, exhaled, a lung
on a ledge, ballooning in the wind's
high whip — we set the corners
with pocked stone, laughed at the thought
of it flung over the edge, blown
like a spore at the two lakes below. We hollowed
out a bowl between scrub pine and
must have struck then tossed every match
in a box before the meshed stook
of dried twigs caught, licked
out, looked over at the opposite face
where sheep like snow-patches slipped
and levelled from crevice to crack.
I heard the moan of fallen arches and
began bad-mouthing the long trek back. Perhaps
we'll stay, push on, higher, west where
the haze of cirrus fades to a passport
black, star-stamped and shut, not just
expat but exhuman; gone hairy, sure footed,
at home with our funk, reading the cairns
of warm dung like prayers before lunch.
I wanted to say something then, just mouth
the option but an old law hung like a beard
in my head. Still unsure: theoretical physics
or high-flown Yeats verse, the thrust
of it was how conditions may
shift from bad toward worse.

Crab

Beyond the sandbar, the sea
was ash-grim, a flint quilt
buckling. Houses huddled, slanting
on the bay's rim like pastel mints on drab
green and granite. Paths
threaded the cragged bluffs
to a thumbnail of beach that was ours
for a summer. Wading through
shallows with driftwood
sticks, we'd lift away shag carpets of kelp
and spot them there — claws up,
scuttling — black eye beads
like cloves looking back as they spidered
away from our toes.

Stacked up in tide pools,
in tangled leg locks, they were
brittle old men, grotesques thrown ashore by the sea.
For hours I gawked at plasticky joints,
spotted, knobbed claws, and
wispy ferns at the mouth, how the sea's lens made
the shells swell, shimmer 'til
perspective was gone and their name
had washed up on my tongue — *Dungeness, Dungeness.*
The boy I was edged closer to them,
brine-spattered, waterlogged, less.

Father Thorne's Bad Saturday

I was behind the church, staking
bean vines when he sauntered up
with the gun. Fringed denim
cutoffs and Leafs-T, he lived

just down from my parish so we'd
go for groundhogs when his father
allowed it. A bright boy, chatty,
I'd laugh aloud at his stumblings

toward God: queries, crotchets as tart
and enticing as new blackberry clusters.
We'd reached the slough in Saar's
south field, hawing at cattle who'd

stare and moan. Chilled fingers meant dusk
was close and we'd shot just the one; I'd
bent over the burrow, a deep eye socket, kicked
the collar of dirt back into its hole, straightened,

turned, and saw that he'd shouldered
and cocked the thing, stood fast with
a held wink. Had trained the barrel-hole
to a spot in my chest. I swear the sun

dimmed to crimson, a cloud-shadow like black
crepe cut the tussocks between us. His name
wouldn't come to my lips. I just dropped the
willow switch I'd been topping buttercups with

and swallowed what spit I had left.

Fighting Space

The revelry ended in a back
alley off Main. Past closing
and well cut, they'd shuffled us
    out the rear door, slumped
    and laughing.
                    We hadn't even
pointed our soggy heads homeward
when he was on us —

    all sinew and knuckle. I could hear
    the chalky grind of his teeth
    as he spat out curses and swore
    he would kill. Shaved head, knotted
    bull-neck, he tore out a
    fistful of Daniel's hair that plupped
    in the gutter: a geeked rat —
    Then, clutching my head and chin,
    stretched back his lips, tried
    to bite off an ear,
                    and was gone —

lost to everyone but himself, a shuttle
that had shrugged off NASA, content to
spin in the unflinching cold
of some further orbit.
Sobered, silent, we headed
home, nursing whatever hurt
        and I remember seeing
it all in slow motion, or
choppy frames of still
life and thinking
he'd gone about it all wrong.
Even as I looked down his throat,
feeling the scene lacked

any genuine fear, was soaked in a certain
pathos, that he'd never perfectly embody
the assassin he dreamed of.

If you hate, stoke a pure hate
and no sidestepping.
If you're simply fucking, call it that,
it was taught you by your father.
If you're truly guarding a diamond
in your breast, compress those
threats to a murmur, cower
and peer inward. Let's settle this tonight —
the stars are all around you.

Waiting on a Transplant

Exhaustion moves in like a mean season.
Thoughts become rigid as teeth, or cattle
in winter, only the steady
steaming proves you're alive.
Bought out by the sheer con of solitude
the year's open mouth looks like a red
room of your own.

         My father now
trundles through the clean halls
of the house waiting on news
of a matched heart speeding over
Alberta in a tin icebox to plunk itself down in the bloody
plush of his chest,
              take up where
it left off, only this time in strange
company, struggling to keep warm
in the Ottawa Valley. Forgetting
the meaning of chinook.

I'm wondering what my father is thinking
as he waits for some young man on a motorbike
to fishtail his way into that dark, blunt syllable,
revving up more cocksure love than either one
of us could muster —

           with my own heart this still,
I'll hear the grinding metal when the Yamaha drops.

Sheep Shed

Not sure it even was a sheep shed;
three squat stone walls, the fourth
formed by the hillface. The stone, whiskered
with vetch, chewed to stubble and corrugated

tin lidding the damp hovel. We'd
scouted the spot in daylight and
returned on this thin road out, the
dark like thick stout, having drunk

just enough to wash us sombre and
awed. Three of us; Kathrin, Maria,
and myself kipping in any abandoned
hut with a roof. We'd swept the packed

dirt floor clear of dung and laid out
a tarp, finally daring to exchange whispers,
with the farmhouse a black bulk down
where road cut through the slope. Flashlight

clicked off, both fists under my chin and
realizing I was not thinking of come-ons
or sex but scared as a child when his
house speaks in the night. Eyes wide as

buckets yawning for light, listening for boots
bearing hard on the trail from house to
shed, the apocalyptic clang on tin
then the steep chase seaward, or —

silence — broad shoulders plugging
the space between lintel and post, blotting
out all but the skinniest finger of moon.
Our tongues pellets of waste with the flock gone.

White Dog

Laura finally found the corpse
after a six-day search.

       Bloated, its fur looking
more like an oily white pelt, it lay
on the banks of the Kispiox River,
its snout a compass needle to the current's pull.
A fist-sized hole pecked neatly
through stomach wall,
                ravens defending
a rope of entrails, like a dew worm coaxed
out on the stone.

We'd followed Laura's weeping, her bent shape
mirroring her dog's on the shale. The two, master and
carcass, seemed like parentheses
hemming in a long red thought —

           Knee-deep in the river, stunned
           in the cold flush that cleaves seeing
           and feeling, I saw salmon dying below
           me, jaws hooking to crimson, bodies in slow
           undulation like spotted mercurial muscle
                and further down, in silt,
           the cycle reopening its mind with a tiny
                but frenetic wiggle.

Later, she asked us to retrieve the white dog
and bury it nearby, though I felt the ravens, black-cloaked
and prosecutorial, had a case
and could be halfway done.

Victoria Harbour

Full, flat sun a loonie in a busker's fez.

Out front of the Empress, a beefeater's
biting his nails in the heat, squinting
at garish white walls of yachts
that tilt in their slips, moaning and
nauseous.

A young boy in deck shoes watches
a minnow flip, for the last time, in
the doughy bowl of his palms.

Cormorants on buoys
are full bottles of merlot,
                    just breathing.
A seal and pup roll
bored, oily eyes on Zodiacs
packed with orca fans —

Nothing backs off,
                    bristles,
      or sniffs.
Nothing bares teeth.
The pup yawns, lays its head
on bleached rubber
                    dreaming of handouts.

Drawing Skeletons

— for Kajin Goh

Living in Cow Head, Newfoundland, you'd draw
bones, collecting them from
beaches and backyards of dead outports.

Skeletal frames of sheep, intact chain of
a seal's spine. The dried,
final frame from a wound up spool, shelved —

sketch the end then drift backward into
an idea of life. Nothing
lives if not in your mind . . .

mites tunnelling the porous bone, awash
in the light of a basement lamp.
You, huddled over a study of humpback's ribs as

a Gros Morne sun sifts through the crackling, black
and white speckled credits.

Sawteeth

Sawteeth rasp through cedar planks,
rough-hewn, seeping
and whiskered at their newly cut butt-ends.

Slapped together as shelving in a cluttered
one-bedroom, they bow under
books, teeter, and test each L-bracket's grip

on the wall. But their alternate function —
fragrance, that express
route to memory where hope chests breathed

strange in the master room, and shavings littered
a cage where a gerbil
was kept, fed, to piss and quiver

under a stunned boy's
gaze until it ran itself out on the wheel.

Wind

stoked and gathering, hoofs it in off
the sea like
a muscled wall, bottled, stalling gulls mid-

flight who hover, stunned, opening
their coats to be
frisked — explodes loose-fitting

clothes, pushes spruce down on one knee,
shoulders up the grey
canvas, and shoves a warmed plug in your

throat so breathing reverses: the lung's bladder
balloons, pressure-locked
long enough to wonder at the effort to believe

voice a treasure

Ex-Con: Friend

On a whim, he'd visit. On a whim. And this was menace.
His jaw set out against the haze
of the upstairs room, grinding his molars
like gear-cogs. His smile was the hull
of a sailboat, white, but thrown in the bad
weather of swollen expression.
Forearms thick as rescue cables, his hands
shook at times and he spoke
openly of this. And up higher, the tattoos, fierce
green maps of the ten years spent
eyeing whitewashed cinder block and
the slow march of chain link.
These were the years when
each man's boot-fall drummed in his
chest, when his transgressions wouldn't leave
him to think, but could fix this in no language
we could understand, we were the terminally
healthy who had never done time.

Then, as suddenly as they'd begun,
his visits came to a halt and relief
flowered over your shoulders, tension
billowed out windows.
The house was yours again
                              and I never said a word of it —

How the moonlight nicked metal
as I chucked the pipe under a shrub,
his hair sticky kelp in the gutter,
swabbing the goo from the curb
(a confidence heating each act as
my mind flew — a spear thrown at childhood
when ethics came easy as alphabet)

then stripped him and washed him down.
Limbs cooling, rolled denim and leather,
slipped them into a bin.
The night was quick and definite.
I lugged his stiffening bulk
with me into your bed then waited.
When you said I was
cold and cuddled closer
that was him,
though he never spoke.

It

Then I, too, opened my mouth to praise —

But a silence wedged my gullet.
— Ted Hughes

It hung there, stiff, and swayed
much as you'd picture a suicide
　　　　　or the moon's bleak appendix.

Though he grew older and was urged
to ignore it, it was never
removed.
Walking, he matched pace with those
around him.
Shat in a porcelain bowl.
Picked flecks from his teeth.
Plotted the y-axis at a polished desk
but never attempted to name it.

In fevered, summer nights when
the walls of his room sweated, leaning
in under plastic F18 Hornets, he called,
　　　　　Mother . . .
and stroking his hair she whispered,
Homo sapien,
it's all I can do . . .

Forced out of his home
he was given ID cards, licences,
given queer looks at his silent,
dusty mouth.
All the while
it hung there and swayed, its shadow
licking his ear as he slept.
He went brittle and ached.
And when it swelled to an unbearable
weight and the sun was a perpetual

gavel banging at the drawn skin
of his temples, he coaxed it down
into a pit, where he lay for
a long time, apologizing.

Notes for His Big Novel

Eight shiny months of AWOL in Truro —
it's all I need — befriend
that surly new dark horse, Leo

and a seam of wrecked wharves,
a mattress, Hudson's Bay wool for covers,

bluffs at the world's lip, dunged-up, treacherous,
an OED and a pocket thesaurus, then

swan dive into the surf
of my youth, soiled and glorious;
chasing the core, no, the pip —
what grew into the truth.

My protagonist, Jim, he'll be thin, reedy,
and potent as the pinner
he smoked on my very first page.
He'll be a sinner. Squandered
his days in bush parties, cow-punching,
backseat lays in chassisless half-tons.
He'll own a gun.

It's all sketchy but framed, planned,
an escape route etched with a stick
in sand. I'll admit the end is in doubt
but we're not half-wits here, we're survivalists —
you figure it out. A main character's fate,
up here, is to saw off his days

in one of two ways: last match, unstruck,
dead-frozen, and whey-faced or racing
to outrun the tidal bore of himself
and always, always only
slightly outpaced.

Officer Warden Unlocks

Fifteen unsmudged years, same squad, in the same force,
far from crooked and not
a bit calloused

but those days of searching — raft-poles prodding in gorse,
hedgerows, and woodlots —
we unearthed

Carla last March who used to do me for free
down a junked alley that
stank of creosote,

sulphur, and beef. I'm not one to grieve
(my wife'll agree, she's seen
ink-eyed calicoes strung

limp from our willow out front) but Carla — to bear her
in pieces, in a zipped up sack, I
sank down on one

knee, felt my marrow wither to chaff, a terror
seep into my skull as
an image — well-framed

but blurred — developed in there of uncuffed lifers
crossing a train-bridge at night.
I couldn't focus

on a fucking thing: the boot-fall, the whispers,
the knife-flicking. It was like
the gates had yawned

open at Penetanguishene.

Micksburg, County Rd. 8

Picture five men in a field.

Suddenly, one is struck dead, driven
        into the mud like a rail spike.

That none of us threw it, that
none of us tossed it into the sky
meant its coming down, just there,
was all the more sinister —

        like a ripped wing panel,
           or cement bird it bulleted,
        went red with its falling.
        The air, naked, molecular, ribbed;
           disintegrating in its
           inability to move fast enough
        toward slipstream.

Six greasy days of flood-rain had hushed
just that morning. The grey
opened like a cardigan to a broad
blue chest and
we stood there, shaky, in couch grass
and furrow, nervous half-smiles, not even
sure we'd earned such sunlight.

  It hit him so hard where
his neck bent it nearly sailed clear through,
pulling the dead face from a foot
of muck, two of us puked
at the squelch.

After questioning, we brought
the children his bowie knife and brass
"Live to Ride" buckle then
took the quick road home.

He Is Helped Along the Way by a Professional

Go on, right here, crack
a sleek sweat and just say it. But
first, rim those pink gums with the nub
of your tongue;

parched, like pumice stone
dragged over pine gum. Now outline
that comma over your eye with
a gnawed down

thumb. Without pause, your whole
body in on the job, hold that set, blue
stare, be Papillon watching his
coconut sack

bob in the crush. Get it over with.
Have it done. Hush . . . eyes off the clock
and do what I do; in a salty,
peculiar, guttural

hum, repeat with conviction, this anti-
prayer haiku:

> *Night. November. I*
> *am alone in New Brunswick*
> *and there is no God.*

Good, and I do hope
it sticks. A cheque will be fine. Should
problems arise — false options, hollow offers —
count to seventeen and then flatly
decline.

Venturing Out

God is too far from God
— Simone Weil

The eavestroughs are plugged
by a corpse the size of a human
kidney; there since spring, pecked at,
and withering. The chimney isn't plumb.
Under scaling shingles a man's brooding
       like a hungry pike bellying
       the sand bottom, a tape loop
       resounding in his shovel-shaped
       head — *lurekillitlure*
killitlure —

A cut in pay and his son never speaks
but that's not it;
tonight his abdomen's hooked, something
wants to draw him out, out of his usual
weeds and sunk willow lair.

Perhaps east side, neon, those faceless
lurking, or just down the park where
rough kids with caved chests

and Jets caps divvy up Dad's morphine.

      A tick and ring race one another
      through the corridors of air vent —

      four walls speak louder than family.
         When stationed at its edge, one can
         articulate space;
                 particular,
        minimal, and dark,

gazing backward to lamplit windows
or a torchlit procession, replete
with march songs and effigies.

In Brendan's Boat

— a letter from Ireland

Frail as ash in a bowl, perhaps
Brendan did make it; faith-sailor.
A voyage that snipped nautical law
like new paper, landing his cloaked
and salted body quivering on the edge
of this country's dirt. Perhaps
he did "predate the Norse" and
glimpsed Labrador's black breathing
arc like the sleek back of a whale
shining through maritime weather
and thought of his brothers,
                                as I do,
in a squirrelly huddle
in their stone church hovel,
as I was in Glendalough, Ireland,
God fading as fast as Brendan, yet
believing his breath woven in wind
combing the backlit hills of heather,
and believing I'll make it back
to spit myself onto the guttural
green rock of Newfoundland's south
shore, where I was born, scouting
the Atlantic depth, the sea floor's crag
and canyon. Skimming the swell, the spray
and wave, bread-crumbing
the journey in gull squawks.

Bonavista

1. From a Photo of My Grandmother

Out back of a house, the blue of a crib
or dorsal fin, the black dirt hoed into
lines, a garden plot big enough
for potatoes and not much else.

This was my grandparents' home, stitched curtains
waving each dawn in time to the tide pushing
out under dories. The men in oilskins,
hardtack between their boots, hack at the bay,
taking nips of good screech to taunt
the bad weather, bolster the guts.

I don't know this village, only its stories.
Did visit once. I was two
when both grandparents dropped
the cove a last grin, whistled
a humpback out of the depth,
and put their leather lives away.

Strongest memory now is a photo:
a two-year-old and his father's mother,
kerchief knotted round the salt straw
of her hair, and a pail
of capelin hinged to her hip.
Mud-caked wellies sunk ankle-deep, we're
spreading fish to rot in the furrows
then nourish the crop. The kid,
one hand splayed, is stumbling
on stubby legs, reaching for the soil
to prop his upper half,
staring the dead catch in the eyes.

2. Mainland Boy In Eastport

Yet when cocky men peered round the curtain of sky
there was no god and the mists came
— Paul Durcan

That cod had come up without effort.
Gavin had hooked its lower
lip and it swam with each hand-
over-hand. Hauling nylon
jig line over the gunnel, beads
of sea water raced away to plop
back into the black.
               Unimpressed, doubtful,
    he kept muttering, *there's nothing on it*
    and his uncle at helm, an eye
    on the water's heave and give, swung
    the boat around, *haul the friggin'*
    thing in if ye felt a tug.

It split the surface and hung there
with the awful, ageless grin
of a bottom-dweller in a dinosaur book.
Gaping and dumb, its filmy eye rolled
then fixed on the jig's chrome flash
stuck through its chin. Gavin slid
fingers under gills, hoisted its cold
bulk over so it thudded on deck;
its white belly, porcelain-smooth,
bumped his boot-toe and expired.

    We tied up at Salvage and went
    home in the truck.
               At dinner,
squeaking his chair across lino,
a mainland boy fidgets while grace
is mumbled through, he's sneering
at the choral amen, at these supplicants,
their decorum, having seen what he'd
raised from the bottom.

3. Uncle In Eastport

Cap-beak smudged with engine
grease, stained denims that sagged
in the crotch. He'd pause, for effect,
then unleash a laugh that bugged
out the veins in his neck. He was all
wrinkles, all pipe smoke and
the same flappy ears as my father,
who he'd elbow with jokes for leaving the Rock,
for having come from away
with these sons who couldn't tell
tomcod from wet socks —

         I buried my fists
in my jacket, squinted into the wake-spray
as the bow banged down over breakers.
Licks of silver mist ribboned
out from the point and beyond that
a damp, blurry oatmeal of grey. Behind me,
he stayed drawn-lipped and hushed,
thick fingers twisting a tin thermos lid,
just doled out two cups — then,
heard through a wind, *I'se a ten-week man . . .*
two kids . . . I laughs when I can.

HEAD INJURY CARD

The Interior

Moss laid a lime rug, quilted
by shade, early spores speckled
the air between columns of spruce. Bears
came out routing the loam, huffing.

     Advancing on equinox, winter's
     stunted days begin to
               expand,
     light cleaving the afternoons
     and the choked cold gush
of the Kispiox.

Returning here for seasonal work,

     where a friend sings elegies
     for a biker who cocked a rifle
     at himself —
opened his chest like a long vowel, spooking
grouse into daylight.

Montana Nocturne

Monstrous night, great wing of no
weight. These stars slotted in chinks
between dark and dark, sequestered,

numb, and undone in the racket of ever . . .

Tent flap. Plains breeze. Pre-sleep's
a cattle guard my mind's caught

its hoof in; here and not
here, how hard I want
not to be isolate — embryonic on

a sage-powdered bleakness where borders
fall back and swarm in in sickening waves and
something like yearning Catherine-wheels out

from its hub under ribs, mouthing
drowsed list of false stops: Heart
Butte, Dupuyer, Troy, and on where

prairie dogs are nervous clerics at prayer
on their haunches, eyeing us
sideways. Soaked in candescent blue

off Dead Man's Basin, we watch frantic
silhouettes on our tent's dim
screen, hear tiny burr-like claws

scritching in grit and this fussing's
a mother blessing our fevered
fall into sleep where our bodies make

covenants and trade heat with the earth.

Westray Dreamscape

Nun-buoy quivers on a seine net,
two trawlers cut the wet
    bonnet of fog, sky sags, world
stands still, holding Nova Scotia
like a bubble under its tongue.

The town seems to cower,
                a clapboard brood
    clinging to that hole in the earth.
All colour subdued,
    as if seen through an ink smudge
or coal dust, ash. Toddlers
wobble then begin to wail. A black
Lab, head cocked, trains its ear
               to a murmur in the crust —

Twenty-six men, their necks bristling,
food in their stomachs and
I was the last
              to see that wall
of daylight recede, to feel my grip
slip from the sprag.

School Bus Broadsided by Patrol Car

First to arrive at the wreck, we moved
like awkward thieves, tender
with apprehension, mouths slits of grim
wonder; as if a huge
           "Do Not Touch"
sign glowed over the mess
like a museum piece.

The children staggered out, unharmed
but fuzzy; cubs from a winter den.
Having been banged awake they kicked
at stones, searched over each other's
heads for anyone taller than them.

           At the cruiser
I looked through the driver's side
at the cop still conscious, sequined
with gemstones of glass shard, he parted
his lips, gurgled, a dark bubble broke
and dripped from his chin.
           The upper half of the other had
sunk into the dash, leaving a cast
of himself, as if the second before impact
he'd been fiddling with the radio, had slid
past a growl of static and
found a clean, whole note —
was remembering his father's violin,
vinyl chairs in a blue kitchen, mother
tapping her foot, and a Tupperware
cup of gin. Managed, *Y'know, when I was . . .*
to his partner before
diving in.

Two Divers Lost, Howe Sound

We'd left the city's thrum and dry
grind to make love for three days
on a bed by the sea

but all night the sky shook,
a dark rug rapped on with sticks.

That navy frigate loomed
up in the strait as if the Pacific had
birthed a naked, new
cliff overnight. Searchlights that leered
from the shells of low
Hueys lit the house with spikes of hard light,
each flare a blind threat,
a goosefleshed glare that preached this third
presence and flattened us
up against our own shadows —

Like escapees in a POW flick we fell —
fumbling with buckles, buttons — into dark
fissures where I'd glimpse your body
in flashes; waxy and sleek, denim
coveralls snaking from hips
like froth off a stone.
    But in that dark space we
    thought of as safety, I kept
    seeing the bloated
    tide-dragged, bumping shoulders
    at bottom in a tea-green murk, their
    air-gauge needles long since
    past Empty, as I went, face first,
for the tunnel.

Deck. It's a Deck.

— for J. H.

It's what I accomplished this week,
then, as if chased, cut a blue streak
to a seat at the bar, where
my kind are par

for the course, and these pints are blinders
strapped snug to the nodding,
hang-lipped head
of a horse.

Wet lime-stink of backfill — excavation —
boulders drilled, split with a sledge, and hefted
like ballast up over the edge.
A trench,

a foundation. Posts and beams, planed
smooth, plumbed, and bolted to — fixed
like monoliths on some island
knoll — then the screams

of a SkilSaw; a quiltwork of tongue-and-
groove sheathing, seams staggered, then
glued. Lengths of bevelled
decking laid crosswise

and screwed. It's what I accomplished. For wages.

Over a gridlock of hedges a house sticks
out its tongue in derision at a house
backing onto its lot whose
tongue is thrust out —

a dark Escher-vision of squarings, levellings.
A plot of middle ground, our own paddock with
centre-post to circle around. We
work and drink and

sweat through unbridled dreams of the mean.

Gotlieb's Column

An afternoon off work bellies
around in the head like
a split melon, green, glistening —
                God, what
does one do when
the weather's immaculate, sweet
as foresight in winter? Buy a *Globe*,

swagger down 8th Ave. past
plaster lawn lions at noon,
pawing and toothy, a spilled

mall cart lies like prey picked
clean or a Catch-Alive yawning
for fat urban coons.
            I sloughed off
my "Focus" section in the first
trash I passed; let her prattle
like rats amid wrappers and tin —

her paid-for trip to Majorca
moulding to fuzz, her day
at the track, his new spats.

The richest banalities shat
out and printed, but fuck it —
today I'm out from under it,
different,
            a puffed-up pleb tightly
                wound, like I could
                    bounce my wan body off
                this tensile light, feeling
buoyed, notorious, Castro's
beard, so full, so sprung
from a trap I could honestly slap
the face off my owners —

Finishing

Every mitre only as clean as the chop saw
it's cut on. Any gouge, puncture, or flaw

in baseboard or casing is quickly forgiven
by almighty Spackle; your putty knife turns uneven

joints into smoothline, turns nickle-sized hammer dents
back into the wood's true profile —
                                        at the owner's expense.

Thin wainscotting strips are worthless poker hands
you keep throwing back to watch land

at attention, soldier-straight, from the bathroom door
right down the corridor's

parade route. That easy. That fast. And if the framing's well built —
no vicious lean, tilt,

or bad wow — the aesthetics should be clear, even simple,
like topping a self-portrait in oils with an eye-pleasing dimple

that doesn't exist in real life.
How else to render a bland, formless grief

into something at least sellable? The mere appearance of beauty's
not beauty, but it's reliable.

Just finish. Get paid.
At night, alone, you'll redeem or undo what your hands have made.

A Winter Carnival, a Moment of Loss

He is standing in daylight, gazing
down at a huge block of ice; a carnival
in winter, hot cider, red sashes, revellers
carving ice block into animation.

He has placed the tips of his fingers
on the frozen surface then closed one
eye, anticipating the cold's journey
up the hard bones of his arm, the way

steam curls around pot handles, up to his
chest encasing his heart. To his left, in
suede and wool, her breath a white round
snare drum, *Yes*

what you feel now is pure, over and over
with the sun in descent. A crowd appears,
his arms jerk back in a bolt of fear, the
closed eye won't open, turns inward as if kicked

and by now the frost has snapped like
a trap on his tongue so there's no saying
why or even I love you. Nothing left but
to chew it. Shadows growing long and a glint

in the open eye, hemorrhaging light into
the dusk, quick, dalliance of motion, now —

Authority

This chill is unmistakably autumn, that
pinching hint of the first gust to strip
boughs, streetlights wear a cut-glass
halo and hum
as you pass. At this hour,
cabbies get reckless, the long, lemon
      sedan leaning
a bend, betting on empty streets, a shudder
and squeal as it straightens,
        moving off —

We have shuffled our lives
to somewhere north of wanting
each other. Used
distance as anodyne. Pared
it all down to these grim-lipped
*take care*s on flint-grey paper. I've
just finished a longish letter
and am walking it off —

      pacing the areas
mapped out for toddlers and well-trained
dogs. The blue cruisers can be seen
in the least likely precincts, prowling
past hedges, inching down backstreets,
roof lights itching to burst.
The alarms are set all over
the neighbourhood,
       and the cops
creep deeper into silence,
onto something.

The Expected

The sky looks afflicted; a sallow, hairless
skull where rain worries
itself to exhaustion and falls. The clouds

are old codgers, belts cinched, bent
at the spine — wheezing —

they lean to shadow the town.

These bowed streetlights like crooked fingers,
their tendons too tight to point or
their skin doesn't fit, drool
electric wax into the snow.

By this glow we trudge through brittle
eyelid cold even dogs won't brave and
convince ourselves home . . . or at least
a front door and mail slot.

From under hedges, cats growing thumbs
whine the wind to a tight riled quiver.
The county's only radio tower has snapped
its bolts near the tip, is transmitting
nothing but coughs.

Winter has lost its footing, stumbles off
blind into accident. All westbound outroads
swallow their signs, choking on place-names . . .

The expected has finally gone wrong.

The Gate
— for S. H.

This verdant rabble, this orchestral
splay of weeds in shade, dandelions
leaning like ushers, like kids with the runs,
and winged ants that taxi then lift, befuddled

as drunks. Swathed in Becoming, in a sprawl
of wild birth, I'm centred on all I've not done;
the solid, sinewy life between shadow and sun.
Here, on rickety, fawn-legged chairs,
                              in this drawl

of heat, our days are these bottles that weep,
diminish, reappear replenished, then fizz,
and silently drain — a shifting fault in the head

to be ever dreaming a calm gauze of sleep
while our thug-dumb bodies plod into pure Is.
Then he set out, and I followed where he led.

What We Didn't Tell the Medic

When the bike dropped it jammed
a foot-peg into asphalt. Blue
sparks spat off chrome, a dead-stop
catapult sent it clear up and

        we slid right under,
        holding each other.

Time stalled. I stared
at the Honda hovering there —
midair — could have sketched
the scraped tank, the locked
sprocket and axle, forks skewy-bent,
wracked wheel-rims, and lolling
headlight eye. It was an ill-framed
Guernica horse strung
up in the sky.

It felt good though, holding
my friend as we spilled onto tarmac.
I wanted to pull his helmeted
head back and kiss him —
for passing those semis,
for muttering *God* as we fell,
for being there with me, ripping south
on the 401 in a stink of coat-leather
burning, arms apart, like he could
wrestle the back bumper
of the Datsun ahead, and that sky,

that ovoid of impenetrable blue,
pressing in, pressing down, the way
sea-swells can pinch a whole ship, just crack
it in two. My eyes flickered, then calmed;
like a deckhand's last glimpse
of the Grand Banks, they caressed
that porthole 'til it sank.

Head Injury Card

Task: to be where I am.
Even when I am in this solemn and absurd
role: I am still the place
where creation works on itself
— Tomas Tranströmer (trans. Robert Bly)

* Unsteadiness on the feet, dizziness

When was. Crustaceans flick tongues in the ocean's ear;

fog clings, marbled. Metal gurney and knees pointed

at cracked plaster. Bite down on air.

Salmon-steak pink. Greased and soft-headed. Alternately

slapped and coddled, coddled and slapped — hands

like talons go for the gyroscope of the eye

* Unusual drowsiness

As if some swell beyond, below the sea's belt

had bone-chilled us, bale-wrapped and banded

our tongues. Sentenced to stillness, a columnar,

wet-hemlock church. A sharp creak sparrows out

from the shed . . . slack-drum thud from the shrubs . . .

It starts in. Pray for its passing

* Mental confusion

Pool of shallow calm, terns two-step in chalked

mist, moist brush of spruce bough. Belong

here, adrift in amniotic flow, this is your . . . no —

I'm at it again, quelling the pain and gush. Semiotic

downpour, onslaught; those first quivering lungs

and no one directing the intake

* Persistent vomiting

Between brown water potholes and clapboard yellows,

lean night halls, over the sea's breaking frown;

a brother. A beach stone. Unreliable air of the world.

Housed in hedged, Ontario towns, every shed savouring its bucked

wood, whimpering collie, cords coiled in a gas-blue

helix of meaning. Basement detritus piling and piling

* One pupil larger than the other

Soccer pitch, clipped, green. Raised on pitches of love

lower than a drone and today, brother, you and I weeping

at the touchline, grass glistens with it. Midfield, a boy

fires off a toy rocket. Zenith, where it wobbles, uncertain,

shies from the thinner reaches, burns up its last, and

shimmies down the ocean we all try to look through

* Persistent or increasingly severe headache

Further back. Feet stirruped, muzzled nurses hover

and grip. Crown of a skull slides out. Algae.

Crown of a skull like the mute in a trumpet's bell and

blow this with your entire, blood-flushed husk. This

music, heard through fog of Demerol, does it flow

into or out from that sea-floor-soft

fontanelle?

MEASURES

I ought never to have taken my lantern to see what was going on in the hut by the granary. On the other hand, there was no way, once I had picked up the lantern, for me to put it back down again.
— J. M. Coetzee

And the trunk was carrying the severed head,
    Gripping its hair like a lantern, letting it swing,
    And the head looked up at us: "Oh me!" it cried.

He was himself and his lamp as he strode along,
    Two in one and one in two — and how it can be,
    Only he knows, who so ordains the thing.
— Dante (trans. Robert Pinsky)

Wolf

Tearing at us flat out, ears pinned back,
shoulders like pistons punctuating air — first
        I thought dog, but one
        look at the paws, their width
        slapping gravel, hinged to spindly
        legs and knew —
spooked, sprinting mid-road toward town.

We pulled the van over and let him pass.
Saw his head bob up, mid-run, to catch
glimpses of barbed fence over the flags
of ditch cabbage. Split
from the pack, hemmed in,
those slit eyes fiercely empty.
He had strayed down onto low ground;
the gasoline and plush, casual
smell of plowed land. Now scanning
the roadsides for a way
                out of the valley, to aged
                slopes where lichen-hooded
                granite cracks loam, trees thin
                to wisps, and shreds of winter slide
                            slow from the tips
of the earth.
I turned in my seat to watch
the blur of hind legs and began
to imagine him collared, tagged,
a noticeable cower in the hang
of his head, pacing a paddock with
some farmer's roan.
Learning to canter —
and next year be groomed.

Wolf Tells

High meadow mind, I am
  scree-slope, dreaming. I pulse

and the hidden population of rodents
  sleeps to this rhythm.

        There is no note — no whiff — here,
    of flesh opened.   I hunt

        this negative, it's why
    I came, to pulse through
        this new, dead stillness and take
            it down. Rip it.

Town, metallic herd. Storm of sound with
    those shapes of heat lazing
        upright in the grey.
                Their young asleep, naked
    bundles of meat-scent under vanishing
    moon, curved bellies wanting; unguarded
            and wanting —
                    I hunt this
        negative. Love
of my lapping where their warmth pours
out. Leave my green

    jaw poised perfect in the grey —

Crow, for the Time Being

Out of the weed-lunged ditch,
    tapered, phlegmatic —
a wet knot — Crow gun-struts
    gunless, an umbilical
of cack-brown, lamentable
      sluice from that ditch

    tautening.

      Stone-chip beak a bone-thorn
in the sun's rib. Squinting, Crow
    wags out of its ditch:

Bachelor. Ex-con. Slut. Crow's

    dark-closet wings cluttered and
    stunning — stunned,
    arctic-blue iron filings wagging
      like fingers, like palsied
        black lashes that blink,

    batting back tears for the
mud-cool, molecular
    plunge of that ditch.

    Not now, Crow —

To Lichen

Something's remains refused
by death, learning to spread; clustered, buckling
   in thin grit. Cling
   and be low, be

sparse as moments of wholeness, treasured
and severe. Scrapings off rock's
inner ear that's heard epochs
   in sound wave striating a sheer
face —

     Cliff snot, brittle
crispness that stays, stays somehow
cloud-coloured, orangish, starved
    green: Dickensian waif-cousin to
    moss, to plush bedding. Oh, granite trying

to be snow, you sleepless, sleep-
proof, trod on and sniffed
    at reverie —

       Stretch.

Nass Valley Lava Field

The fox did not enter me —
   just flicked a red ear
   that funnelled my
   breathing then slid into
      the thicket like wind.

So I've laid myself down
   on this loam-damp crust, lace
   drop cloths of lichen cradle
     my spine and I'm listening
   to deep taproots etching
their dramas through
subsoil, the faraway tinkle,
   like pearls come unstrung,
   of pupae hatching in slag.

       From down here,
bundled stooks of lodgepole
pine point through blue
   to a chipped, white
   dish I've lapped patience
from all through the winter. How

   can I not forgive the months?
   They've weaned me
      on bone-cold, brought
    me here hungry — half-grown —
a heavy-lidded squabble of cells,
a grin-and-bare-it Prometheus
   hearing his eagles emerge
    like sprigs from the dirt, from
   dead hollow cedar-rot, sun-burnished
    chapels of grass.

         The chattering legions.
         The thousand-eyed — mouths so
   tiny this feast may
   just go on forever,
   this banquet bury us all.

Ice Fishing on the Ottawa

The fishing shacks have emptied
themselves of hooks, heaters, and men
and now stand propped against drifts,
creaking at the arrogance of stacked
lumber on the shore.
      The molecules of night have
      slowed, nearly chilled to a halt
      in the locked jaws of December.
Only the sound of a truck
reaches you. His rig shudders, moans,
moves off, a beast busting the contract
of silence out of sheer loneliness.
He'll lunge at the Trans-Canada,
skirting the Ottawa, bleeding Pembroke, Cobden,
Westmeath of their youth. He'll grip and crank
the wide wheel, force his grill against time,
pass crags of cutaway granite looming
up in his beam, his zippo lid's click
ticking off miles, eyes reddening as
he hauls the whole load toward
dawn's red bloom. The rest of Ontario
sleeping like pike under ice.

What to Do about Dinner

Two pounds of mussels lugged back in a bag
tocking like castanets at the hip. If
they make you think
as they tumble steamer-ward,
of derivations from fruit — odd
conjugations of fruit — it's of fruit's shadow: shadow
of peach, of almond, of clamped,
unyielding anti-fig.
Even the juice smells of coastal rock and
wagging, limp but unmovable kelp; a grim
life clustered under Port Aux Basques fog.

Prying the lung-shaped shell
a fraction of the sea dribbles down
your hand, the heart is flung away
from dinner conversation to bloom
alone. Cracking
the sinewy joint, exposing
cooked flesh, now tinged
with ginger and twisted from the heat —
                    a delicacy, even
when fruit is in season. Grin.
Everything's mother-of-pearl.

Flea Market: A Love Story

One Saturday in a million, midwinter,
when you know you're in love. She,
zinging like a pinball in bumpers
from stall to loaded stall, and he,
cliché about a cookie jar
or himself in a bar.

That powder blue, 1958 Hoover upright.
A stately die-cast metal
number with a roving Cyclopean headlight
and toe lever we could settle
on hi, low, normal, or shag.
A detachable spring-hook bag.

The vendor packed our plastic and steel
trophy into his van — afternoon dark-berry-
jam light squished between its Mason jar seal
of cloud and new snow — then ferried
us home for nothing more than a handshake.
Through teary rear windows, bloated flakes

like packing-crate polystyrene puffs duned
and drifted the world a futureless, stop-motion
white. Horse-blanket comfy. A pair. In tune.

We sucked up what we should've aired. Our plug-in
prize pony winters in a choice spot near the furnace.
The cost of its feed, enormous.

Night Portrait of B., Asleep

Fronds of pulled toffee
on a china plate

Two tiny feathers under
sideways apostrophes

                              A spider, belly up
                              with a twitchy leg

A shy slight wind over white stones
that sounds like elsewhere
                    or Elsinore

Twin models of the Kremlin,
one sliding off to the left

Ripples in pressed sand

A chocolate drop, a knot
in the centre you can't undo

This arrowhead sheathed in kinked moss
and the whole canvas a gradual wash in blue

Steady

Mind in its purest play is like some bat
That beats about in caverns all alone,
Contriving by a kind of senseless wit
Not to conclude against a wall of stone.
— Richard Wilbur

Suicide. The phone call turns us idiot; you gasping
at new wind-walls of grief and I speechless; wooden
as doorjambs, dim in the abhorrent calm. Who
were we moments ago? What distance from love's
gorgeous ruckus hovered even the notion of it?
Otter and otter, slicking love's mudbank, thatching
our thoughts like rushes to smoothstone, cress — our tools
of play are what hold us, moor us belly-to-earth
or tugged, tumbling in a current of this and that.
Mind in its purest play is like some bat

As we set ourselves to small tasks (turning chives
so they fawn toward light, finally framing that postcard
from Kiev) and the scraping, the clanging of tactile life
loosens the solemn knot that's clogged up your wonder —
"Is an hour taken, even a minute, to measure love?" Measure,
weigh in, or a series of simpler functions; throwing
breakers, shutting valves on a summer cottage reduced
to a box-shaped bunker for winter. Deliberately scripting
his heart's notes from warm, layered fugue to a monotone
That beats about in caverns all alone,

forever emitting this chill but long since past listening.
Crimson valentines, white trim snipped from doilies, public
school sweethearts, you learned together, and early, the first
tinkerings of sharing one's self, and that rarest of gifts:
the love that survives youth's bat-blind, rigorous stretchings
to plant itself intact in the soil of maturity. Then long
absences. Laced liquor and cocaine hazing self-hate while he
shattered himself in Hull's loneliest clubs. You saw
him through even that. Flagrant destruction didn't stick,
Contriving by a kind of senseless wit

to guide each other an inch closer to health when
the black hours hit. I must owe him so much —
your exquisite listening, those echoing wells of endurance,
equally yours and his, where I now fill a cup tipped and
emptied so often. Amazed, in love, I laze
with our cat watching you sift through last things:
birthday card, a short note in a proud, thick,
felt-markered script — yes, weigh in, feel scales search
out their balance, a river's poise is sorrow's home —
Not to conclude against a wall of stone.

Conversation Fragment

She says: Seek help! *Ha-ha Ha-ha & Christ.*
— John Berryman

Between friends, often what's felt's never uttered
or we're muffled, elk-dumb, then herded
to a private grief-pasture to putter

and suck. "Anyone manages that, I'm ecstatic" sounded
tragic, an acquiescence to boredom, an admission of lack —
Sorry, S., but my mother is sad, and dogs bounded

through a dream where my father's mind's crack
yawned to a chasm, full echo, dial tone (frets
on the same neck). Like flushed quails, odds stack

against us if we bolt at first stirrings, vague threats.
Some thespian voodoo: don't mention the Scot
or ride your heart's swing to the corners of its

grin — it's then blood recalls its own power to clot.
I'm outside myself with thanks that you called
but wish you were elsewhere, Texas perhaps, caught

by the cuff on the quills of vast places, stalled
in sunlight, forced to write. To qualify,
mediate, lie. My father's a shit, S., old, bald —

Christ, there's no knowing when or where or how or why.

". . . Resigned to a Quiet Life"

Private room, squared to the night world, where
I was buried in the burlesque of a letter
that felt important, like a thin inner cord
being untangled and when finished, would better

my grip on the wherefores and whys. The gas fire
exhaled in blue whispers as if shushing the furniture,
or wowed by the Druidic text of shelved books on crop
failure, maybe, or alchemy, or how young beasts mature.

A quiet so silky, protective as river silt, I felt immersed,
turtled in think-mud as I explained to this friend
how I'd taken to heart what he'd said about preparedness
resembling so closely its opposite that, in the end,

any precaution only comes as a shock. Then, without
warning, the phone wailed — scaring me clear off my seat,
the upswing on my *g* in "resigned" shot
off, tearing a diagonal ditch through the sheet.

I picked up, screw-eyed in the dark, as if woken
from sleep, as if stunned back to life with a ringing
slap. Nothing. Not even dial tone. Just echoing, hollow
hum from some presence refusing to speak and this bringing

me round to my own presence; the gooseflesh and
fierce need to piss, the pain of my ear folding
back under pressure of silence. I remembered a pact I'd
made as a boy: to answer indifference by withholding

love. *You can fuck off, whoever you are* . . . feeling
not just ignored now but watched. It was all too
scripted, staged, like I'd just lived some modern fable
whose moral was the returning of the mouthpiece

to its cradle.

f-Love, or
Caught My Love in My Hand

Yes, it was autumn, Indian summer, and eight cowbirds
pack-hunted one mate in her flight.
Yes, I was kneeling, a supplicant, white eyes upturned
to the coruscating, seal-deep onyx of night
            and I would love
to be able to honestly say it was you,
or a marigold-scented semblance of you,
who arched in my head, catlike, gasped
then cooed, but a vast, dim plain like
Montana or the face of the moon
unfurled instead — soulless, expectant.
Then I burst and emptied into the flat
of that land, the sum of my oneness —

an opaque roux, an amorphous
puddle like those that gulls drop in sand.

This isn't my love I've caught in my hand —

not love,
but a potential
reincarnation of Ayn Rand.

Heaps of Broken Bottles Glitter in the Sun

— after Mark Strand

Age ten was a carnival tent but mobile,
scouring the town's hem for hubcap, trophy. Servile

and driven by the nip and bay of our dogs, we
dance-stepped the field's hailstone memory.

Calibans with a bird in each shoe. Though
the heart tingled at the sight of blood,

for a short time the seasons spun on an axle
of games and rode joy to an unleashed

plunge — everything given at birth, proffered
to new hands like a talent for landscapes,

a headful of steam, then locked away
as we grew to know solitude. Alone

with the roulette rattle echo, we scour
each city's papers for news of our

own passing. The photo, the August night
we'll recognize as counterpoint

to the perfumed dirge we've become —

that kiosk counter at chest level and
the softball's taunting, sponged heft,

the funk of moneyed adults
in sneakers and thongs, their candied

breath a dank mould on your nape.
Peering into the shadow and pall

of a games tent where rigor mortis pandas
noosed on fishing line, levitate over

the coin box — fat, seamless — their eyes
like larvae under glass, and you've

targeted the gap in the grin of one clown
where he shows plywood and pressboard

under greasepaint. Your knees, coltish,
clang an arthritic ache, erode onto

tarmac, and shake. Pinch
back a burr of sobs in the throat

                  and just throw
into risk —

             A man grunts.   Shuffles off.

Night pulls pegs from the heart's clay, feeds
slack to tie-lines, billows, and puckers

in the dust. With a bankroll of gold opiates,
morning outbids all comers.

Favourite Player

Tongues lilying out, our boots slowly froze
in the drifts, their laces like mouse tails
printing the snow. It was a hike

to that lake and first skating out,
clearing off snow with oven-curved
stick blades, fevered the wait and furthered

the heckle-filled pause of pre-game

to a light-glare tensing of love for
these friends at your back; the *fuck off*s
and yelping at smacks from their sticks.

Ankles wobbly, weak as wet cardboard,
you almost willed them upright until
the gliding shave of sharp turns gripped

both your legs, and speed became
a kiss that the rust-peppered blades
and thick, ticking ice shared

for themselves. We chased a stray

puck off over the bank, Derek and I;
heat-flushed, still in our skates, knocking
through crisp, tawny bulrushes, thigh-deep

in cold glitter and stumbling

and steaming —

steaming —
it whorled up off him as he plunged
in a mitten to grip it.

First Lesson in Unpopular Mechanics

As a boy, it was a scale-model Messerschmitt
pitched at the wall in a boy-scale rage —
Now? These grown-up middletones, wafflings, shit
flung deliberately wide of the fan. I remember the age
I began to ease off — thirteen, fourteen —
when busting one's stick meant a five-minute major,
and there, in the sin bin, thinking, *what did I mean
by two-handing the crossbar?* Couldn't gauge or
properly reckon what point I had made (hoped
I had made) so kept my caged gaze on the raftered clock:
that massive, red-rashed, free-floating block
where the seconds of my sentence, my stasis, loped
toward zero, zero, and zero in slow-mo.
The thing opposed, absolutely, my re-entering play; its rules,
                                        its flow.

To a Sister, Wherever

Why should I recall that brush you were beat
with for your fourth lie that week? Control
abandons the pious and scrubbed who eat
in thick silence, whose fists, tongues only unroll
when they're praying . . . Christ, it's so easy now
to look back, analyze, judge, or deny
but I was there — watching — whispered *ow*
to myself as the welts boiled up on your thigh.
Bright-lit, bristling kitchen of angles, hair liquid coal
above stainless-steel chair legs, the linoleum lifting. How
to account for these visitations in daylight? Objects —
their imprints — stack up, grow like a subsurface reef.
Sister-ship, sister-swimmer, our estrangement connects
us. I hope you're well. I've found sleep a relief.

Shadows

This was during a drought
in Essex County I have no
record of except the feeling of dust
in the teeth and
                    all the green gone
out of things.
Young, lustrous-headed, leaping
the stream, energy running slow
through stretched hours —
                 the bow
my own hands crafted, taut, strung
this way like a bent, hard hope
             and the bulrushes, cattails
as arrows tracing their high flaming
parabola, burning close to invisibility
in the blind eye of the sun.
               Then the grass
igniting, charred shadows chasing
us into chaos, into the game gone wrong.
    Escaping to the rusted CN railyard,
    into the tree house, planks
    chewed, wasted by decades and
    red rot. And in my climbing, I nudged
a claw hammer that found,
with an eerie exactness, my brother's
head where he waited below and met
him where his hair parted —

            all of us silent, then,
          as a thing in flight. All of us deep
       in shit if we ever make it home.

2

I suppose it's there now, set
        in my memory. The spikes
driven into the tree, cross planks,
the burden of a mistake carried on your
shoulders. My father's Protestant stain
            on my heart; a child
peering wide-eyed at pain, at blood
                bubbling into gun-blue clots.
      I'd rather speak here
          of other things.
That clean, perfect numen that was a stoppage
of time as the cattails burned, and my throat
like scorched earth pinned
      between fear and a howling
     laugh when the hammer hit.

How that hammer found its mark
from forty feet. The world's stunning
authority
        that ended our fun.

The way a mother can snag a lie from your lips
    with her hands in dishwater.

3

At a young age
and by accident, it comes to you —
some games are lost at their outset,
a burned patch defies seasons
        and renewal.

Now on the Pacific coast, B.C. Day, watching
the violet and ochre burst, the rooster-tail
frenzy of rockets, their hissing
   climb to a sky raining
      umber and gold. Each arc
twinned in the harbour's black pane.

            I'll linger awhile, as crowds thin out,
               to see what remains, what's left
            in the dark after
            colour is spent.

Angle

Bamboo wood chimes have sung themselves
into an inert knot,
a complex mobile I never had the patience
to untangle as a child, rather chose to
stare into its webbed mess
                  and give it credit.

Such less-than-perfect grain runs
the length of a life.

Stripped threads meant a bike seat
would never tighten —
    A father who played no sports, who
    once broke a toe sprinting the length
    of a backyard —
        A chemistry set without explosives, not
        even a kid-sized bang —

This living feels like a low-ceilinged
basement, the damp, the unused gallons
of flat white, a wrench gone missing,
and through a storm window, the ground-
level view of the earth.
                  A garden sprouting
new chives, pumpkin sun, community of ants.

Signature

He sat on the rock and was still,
still and his surface glittered
like mineral. No waves at a river's edge,
so all is sieved and sucked out,
slightly bemused as a memory skitters
on the surface, a water bug whirling
in search of anything smaller than itself.

Here, where the Muskrat seeps
into the Ottawa like a wise old ditch,
he'd seen herons, poised,
elegant as reeds, netted
with the shadow of willows. Their otherness
an agreement of patience, watercolour,
and unlikely curves.

He sat with his pulse. The lighthouse
a congruent blip on the periphery.

*

Having once been employed as marina
security, I was to comb the hundred
or so yards of river beyond the breakwater,
to lash up and tow any deadheads
                    ashore, at least mark them.

In an aluminum soap dish I'd careen
the night water, only at night, moving
out and away from the docked yachts
in a stitched pattern, trailing behind
me the rattly hum of the outboard.
Like a cicada in thick woods or
a bad idea, I couldn't be
                    spoken at —

Often, with the black a cloak
on my shivers, I'd spell my name
in the oily sheen; a transient signature
in current rushing east

                    where the river condenses —
          its ribs squeezed, girdled by granite,
          heightens to a roil, rapids slurring
          their speech over stone teeth
                    in a surprise torrent —

     shallow and mad, as if eager
     to spread, finally,
     to deepen with importance again then

drift, hapless, brindled silver and coal,
into the capital, heaving
all its strange carp toward Parliament.

A Leave-Taking

1

As you walked, night grew, grew into its boots,
plum blue into pungent pine mat, meadow.
Feeding on asphalt and the electric
current of swollen crickets, night ate
while your own eyes starved. Ditches rose
up, swallowing fencing — posts, phone poles,
attending thicket all thickened to black.
Annihilation breath-close and towering,
like putting an eye up to knotholes
in barn walls. On concession roads
you made concessions to fear —
                    I can walk as far
as the footbridge, I can walk as far —
a prayer that seemed transmitted from
your fist where it hung, where a stone
from the underfoot gravel warmed in wet
folds and stood for a smallness worth
arguing with. Coached on, reined in
by a sideline of megaphoned, gross-throated
frogs. Soft moth panicked your hair then
flits off, is gone; in the uncommon sway
of night's greatcoat, perhaps never was, but
a tingle awoke, travelled down the weed
of your spine, and your inner ear's fugged
with by the off-time scruffings of other,
invisible, oncoming boots . . .
Offer your hand, your stone, mute, huge
with new regions.

2

El Camino, Firebird, Nova; they'd growl
in a huddle, owners on hoods picking
out fags under sulphurous lamps while
Airborne on leave bristled and thugged

through the clubs clutching money —
a buttoned-down, Jordache, let-God-sort-'em-out
set. Stand too close you'll hear
cartilage pop in the trapped reek

of cologne. We'd pin our eyes to bourbon-
hued carpet, cower, duck out early, and
get drunk under bridges: no-see-ums, black-
flies, midges sank in the gin and we'd

wince at the burn of that cocktail —
three parts boredom, one naked rage. Drop
acid. Rinse. That town where we hid was
infected; a boot camp,

a cage

3

Over Shield rock edged like a dolphin's back
you watch woods, walled, rattling past
and the rolling wake of bruised sumac.

You've hitched this ride from a lumberless lumber
town, rifling change off the dash, tape
deck cranked, the number of

cigarettes left in your pack is a symbol —
or plain fact, either way, it recurs in
your head like a chant so you keep on.

And it's this nimble cat-stepping between
the brash urging of what is, and the constant
soft shoulder approaching, widening, converging

again back where these woods strangle or corset
the road. You're young. You need nothing.
All that's behind you is shitty. A spore,

a seed that finds its own transport, breaks
itself open on deadpan, impoverished clay:

city _____

4

A remnant rusted to a papery
thinness, shaped
like those masks worn to masquerade

balls, but in metal with eyeholes and
all. Its skin of black
paint has chafed, lifted, bubbled

away in spots revealing tired russets,
corroded reds veined
and blotched with lighter shades closer to

gold. *Northern Ontario Road Metal*, it's
called, the artist
mounted this oxidized grimace on a bright

orange field, under glass, and gave it
to me last Christmas.
What is it? Where is it from?

Being older he smiled, held his tongue, watched
me clamber and grope
for some meaning to pin to this *bright obvious*

standing motionless in cold. Live with and enter
its surface, texture of old
drainpipe or cow's tongue, colours made

loud by their background — I relive the loud
rash the Ottawa River
broke out in each fall, its tattered banks stitched

up by woodpeckers with a cicada's shrill thread.
The roads drifting
out of that town were all golds, reds, and

rot splintering the heads of greying posts.
Each dead farmhouse
alone in its proper plot, made beautiful by cold

light and long shadow, our dreams put on edge by
what each house lacked.
Detritus. Remnants. A scrap salvaged and

kept as reminder: Don't always look back —
but look back.

ACKNOWLEDGEMENTS

Many of the poems have appeared previously (often as younger likenesses of themselves) in the following publications: *The Malahat Review, Fiddlehead, Matrix, Canadian Literature, Quarry, New Quarterly, The Dalhousie Review, Grain, Sub-TERRAIN, PRISM International, Poetry Canada Review, TickleAce, The Antigonish Review, Queen Street Quarterly, Written in the Skin, Vintage 97–98,* and *Riprap: Fiction and Poetry from the Banff Centre for the Arts.* Thanks are due to the editors of each.

Deep thanks to everyone at The Banff Centre for the Arts — not least of all, the bartender with the Uncle Tupelo and Wilco albums.

For their professionalism, warmth, and confidence in this book, I owe much to Martha Sharpe and Adrienne Leahey at House of Anansi Press.

Jeff Hardill, Suzanne Buffam, Tamas Dobozy, Steven Heighton, John Donlan, Kathrin Zinkmann, and Laura Panter have all been to me: friends, readers, family, loves, and, in the case of Hardill . . . Hardill. I can only hope they know . . .

My editor, Don McKay ("UncleLear"), deserves all the credit for transforming a bunch of almost-poems into a book.

And finally, to Barb Panter, who is what I seek daily, all love.

Quotations on page 1 are from "The Polaroid Memorandum" in *Landslides: Selected Poems 1975–1985* by Don Coles and "Joe Soap" from *The Price of Everything* by Andrew Motion. Used by permission of McClelland & Stewart, Inc. *The Canadian Publishers,* and Faber and Faber Ltd., respectively.

Quotation on page 17 is from "The Scream" in *Cave Birds* by Ted Hughes. Used by permission of Faber and Faber Ltd.

Quotation on page 26 is from "O Westport in the Light of Asia Minor" in *The Selected Paul Durcan* (Thistledown Press, 1989). Used by permission.